Lyrics of Reason
&
Experience

Munyaradzi Mawere

Langaa Research & Publishing CIG
Mankon, Bamenda

Publisher:
Langaa RPCIG
Langaa Research & Publishing Common Initiative Group
P.O. Box 902 Mankon
Bamenda
North West Region
Cameroon
Langaagrp@gmail.com
www.langaa-rpcig.net

Distributed in and outside N. America by African Books Collective
orders@africanbookscollective.com
www.africanbookcollective.com

ISBN: 9956-791-39-3

DISCLAIMER
All views expressed in this publication are those of the author and do
not necessarily reflect the views of Langaa RPCIG.

Dedication

To Prof Francis B. Nyamnjoh
For stimulating my thinking
and for all his mentorship
and scholarly inspiration!

Table of Contents

You

You and trouble are brothers if not sisters
Twin sisters
Or better twin viruses

You!
You don't know when to choose
Sometimes you choose the wrong time
Not because you are disgusted with our being
But because you don't know when to choose

Like sea wind
You don't know when to blow
Not because you hate the sea
But because you don't know when to blow

Like a tree seed
You don't know where to emerge
Not because you have no feelings
But because you don't know when and where to choose

Like mad waters
You don't know where to flow to
Not because you love demolition and plundering of property
But because you don't know where to direct your energies

Like the mentally disturbed
You wonder about and visit all places
Not because you love all places
Or respect all people
But because you don't know where to visit

You
The best buddy of trouble

The New Generation

When I cry myself hoarse
Who on this land will hear my weak voice?
When I sing myself hoarse
Who on this land will pay heed to my unfinished song?
When I call myself hoarse
Who on this land will hearken to my hoarse voice of wisdom,
the message of our unfinished business?

Our hearts
Elders
Are heavy
Replete with much sorrow
Caught on prevaricated crossroads

Penetrating deep the labyrinth of the hearts of our youths
The leaders of the day tomorrow
We see only sluiced conscience build around crucibles of mist
smoke

Their minds
Chartered with the vertigo of westernization
That our forefathers condemned in their loud voices
Never would they dare imagining chasing the western ghettos
of the day
And these odd cultures writhed in manacles of globalization
Harbingers of bad omen on the land
Upland by the Rafraf hills
Thick forests of miombo woodlands have become a desert in
the measure of a second
The wetlands in the east have been helplessly marooned

On the other side of the hills – there
Our ancestors have been cursed
Their burial shrines are now suburbs of the western style
The night now never fall
Flowering girls never sleep even a minute
Following the seditious rays of the new sun that never sets
Only to be stubbornly harvested raw
Shattering hard the dreams of their forefathers

Our generation heaves a sigh of change
Fragrant nostalgia of lived hazy maze of our childhood
Now scratching the back of our heads all day
Taking stock of our good that so far has perished
In the guise of what is their best
Our worst
Only regrets

Continue on your Road

This is the time
The onset of a protracted revolution;

The sun is rising, rise my son, rise with it!
For this is the time to rise

Through perseverance and courage the sun has travelled through darkness
The rays of the long day are spreading before you with dazzling brilliance
A sign for good hope
Yet the journey still lies long your way

Start now then, start
Your protracted journey of struggles of good hope

There will be scorching heat along your way
With tinkling rays penetrating deep to your bones
Courage!
That is time to rise

What do you do when danger approaches and there is no way out?
Stand up on your feet and face it
Even with sidekicks from all directions
Stand up
Courage!
For that is time to fight

There will be thunder and hailstorms
Tornados and cyclones of all kinds along your way
With harsh, surly weathers
Persevere!
Continue on your road
For that is time to walk

Even when weather subsides
Bringing in you comfort, peace and calmness
For one moment in your journey, remain vigilant:
Of the comfort given to you to replace your sufferings
Of the shelters offered to you to cover your body from harsh
weathers
Of the clothes offered to you to replace your rugs
Of the smiles offered to you to replace your tears
For that may be time set for you to fall

Should you fall:
Be disheartened not
Rise with elegance without looking at the face of your
enemies
Or back but forward ever
Continue on your road
With reinvigorated zeal
Go!
You will get there

Looming Tornados

I looked carefully
Listening attentively
When I first heard the sound of the approaching tornados

For a moment, I pondered for the next step forward
There were numerous spaces – empty spaces in my heart
Worse still in my thoughts
All had crumpled from an internal tremor
But still harbored in the dungeons and crevices of my nerves
for postmortem

Tanita contemplated assuming responsibility
But that was not her
Neither was it John
Nor my grandma

As usual grandma worried looking
Carried away in voyages and forays of imagination
As day passes, night falling
But my persona still wrapped hard in darkness

Surely fierce tornados were looming
Looming, looming, looming!

Knocking hard on the door of my heart
I could feel the smell just by the door
As I see her - herself in her unusual mood
A white paper in the right hand
Her pace that of a dejected soul
I could feel my blood simmering

My nerves numbed
My eyes all tears – cloudy and misty
For the looming tornados had now arrived

Broken Hope

It remains there printed at the back of my mind
Hidden but blatant
It hangs
Your untimely departure
A warmth touch

A glimpse to the past
A capture of runaway thoughts
Prowling like mad bulls

Your thinking, my thinking
An invisible resemblance
Connected to each other in a cobweb of networks

Now the connections only shadows
Blank, buoyant – weighed down by melancholy

Though I need them reconnected
Hopelessness simmers
Blowing the steam of connections further away

A Servant of Love

It is love and only love
That made my heart chooses
To follow you physically and in spirit
Everywhere you are I am present
Day and night
For my love is larger than the sea

This love barged into my heart
Like man-made lightning of the witch
Shook the walls of my arteries
And fondled the walls of my pulmonary vein
All my heart is invaded
I am a servant
Or rather a captive

I have changed my step
To suit your pace
I have changed my dance
To suit your rhythm
I have changed my song
To suit your tune
I have stumbled along strange paths
To win your favours
I have blinded my eyes
To absorb all the love you radiate

Faithful love is blind
Many times it is coward
Unkind
And even unfaithful

With all the rumours
Even my noses smelling the rat
My tongue made dumb with the lies of your lips
And part of me longing to resist
My ears refused to hear
My eyes refused to see
My heart refused to heed
For now
I am a servant
Held captive by love the conqueror

The Silent Violent Night

Facing east
Glaring, a glimpse to the west
With cloudy sorrow eyes
Yearning for the runaway sun

Stuck for a moment
Contemplating
Peeling the silence of the dark night
Layer by layer
Like a mother decorticating an onion
Silent

Then the night violent wind
Chaotic
Whips up the dark colored night
Asking for the moon's whereabouts

I mourn in grief
For the moon

And I yearn for the sun
To bring its dazzling rays
And spill its warmth
For everything to be alright with the world
For peace to prevail to all
For love to plant its roots
And for comfort to be enjoyed by all

Sinful Old Man

He fluffed up them away
Calmly as with love

To them he presented
Notes of all currencies
Cars of all models
The high class cell phones
And low density suburbs of Centurion

Deep in his heart he was singing
A funeral dirge for the catch
For he had been given the allowance to taint

An old little devil
They envied
His round handsome face
His sex stealing eyes
They all ran amok in forays of imagination
Running up and down in voyages of an explorer
Clinging on his broad shoulders
Carrying themselves into his thoughts
For they fathom nothing more than his masquerades of a
Good Samaritan

By freeing themselves
Alas!
Devil's romantic tale
Jolly yells
Battered with wonders of madness
To the boxes without space

They all find themselves
Cold
Still for good

A Short Love Poem

I

When I look into your eyes
I see two rays
A ray of comfort
And a ray of good hope

II

When I think
I doubt not
That God was wise
To create man and woman
Let alone to live in a near-far world
Where He could watch
The virtues He planted in men

III

I will not leave you
Wherever you go
When you go
Go with your body
Your spirit
I behold in your honor

IV

When I die
I swear
I want them to bury me in three graves
In God's palace
On mother earth
And in your heart

V

Te day I first talked to you
At 1 am I slept
So overwhelmed by the imprints of imagination
I saw myself in your long lovely arms
Resting

VI

I remember that other day
My sister by my side
Snoring
I dreamt awake
Seeing you – your lips stealing away my saliva
I woke up
To embrace your gesture
I couldn't see you

By the whirlwind of the night
You had been blown away
To a place
Far far away

Beckoning
You couldn't see
Calling
You couldn't hear
For my voice
Was like a whisper of conscience

There
I sat
My soul dejected

My sister awaken
By the sweetness but desperateness of my voice
She couldn't recognize me
For I was for you
All myself

VII

When I slept again
God commanded
That you come
Give me a lovely hug
That I ever longed
That you pose for a sweet kiss
That I ever longed
That you dress me a wedding gown
That I ever longed

VIII

Alas!
My God is good
He granted me all this freedom
To love
Even when not loved
To think
Even when nobody thinks about me

He
Is so wise
For to us
Who love
He whispered:
'They win only those who play'

I played
Today
We are together
In this lovely love nest

Geriatric Testimony

Years and years ago
When the stars were not yet born
When donkeys used to have horns
And rocks raced against each other
We used to go out at night
Out in the moonlight
To play
And to dance

We were boys and girls of all ages
Who knew that when gray leaves fall young green leaves take
a cue
Some from that village across the river
Am forgetting its name
Ah I remember!
Makwama
When time for song came
We would all speak in songs
That was our language
Oiled with whistling willows
Of our boys' glorified tongues

The turn for dance
We would all speak in dances
That was our language
Oiled with melodious ululations
Of our girls' glorified tongues

But that was years and years ago
When donkeys used to have horns

And rocks raced against each other
In competition for a win

Now
Moonlight come
Moonlight go
No sign of life in the village
For all life is dead
No dance in the village
For all dance is dead
No play in the village
For all play is dead
Yesterday is dead
I am speechless!

One day
I ask: why?
They tell me all sorts of stories:
Westernization
Sparkling globalization
Formal education
Television
General disregard of mother culture
Again,
I am speechless
For gone are the days

You will Never Know

I am wasp without sting
Bee without honey

I am concept without meaning
Life without reason

I am bird without wings
A donkey that flies

I am bad news
The playmate of tears

I am sorrow that laughs
The friend of sadness

I am trouble that searches
The friend of danger

I am child of the sea that roars in summer
All that comes across I devour without mercy

I am happiness that glitters
The buddy of love

I am nothing that boasts
The son of vacuum

I am scorpion
The sting master of all enemies
I am MAA'T forgotten in the temple

The lover of peace

I am gold in the mine
A treasure left idle in the valley
I am salt the preserver
I am vinegar the enemy of germs

I am mayhem
The lover of confusion

I am war the lover of demolition
The harbinger of bad omen

I am a Good Samaritan
The friend of those in need

I am a teacher
The lover of wisdom

I am who what you don't think I am
The son of stupid imagination

So,
You will never know what I am
Guess

Lamentation of the Hero's Wife

In forays of imagination
In sojourns of solitude
I wrestle all day, all night
Always thinking of him
My hero
Our hero
But unsung

At your funeral
Funeral of the unsung hero
My departed lovely Loveall
I heard stinging words I dare not speak
I smelt scent I dare not smell
I danced to the songs I dare not sing
Only for the sake of your orphans
Otherwise they wanted me to accompany your even to the
ancestors

I remember your song
That lovely song to all
'Justice the cause of my fight
Love the cause of my fight
Peace the cause of my fight
And survival the cause of my fight'
Even though at that time
Strife was the order of your day
And treachery your daily bread

Even together
We had the song we sang as a family

But I dare not sing here
For fear of the ears of the air
And eyes of the trees

That song
Perhaps I will only sing
The day I join the line
And for now
Let us only make merry
There
In the motherland of figmentation
A free land for all

Though with only one eye
Like a tadpole
I should remain vigilant of the fish eagle
Like a rat
I should remain vigilant of the cat

My heart though a threadbare
The whiff of you teasing me eternally
Diffused in gray steaks of sorrow
It befits not
That I join the line now
For in earnest I still need to fight
For the peace you always preached
The peace all your people very much longed

Chocolate Star

They say I am a star born of black
But I insist I am a star born of chocolate
For to me the reality of color matters
But when I say this
They say I am too political a poet

Well,
Like the cognoscenti of all that masquerades as white
I am full of blooming hope and dazzling radiance
Perhaps even more

How can I shine in the day
If I am a star born of black?
How can a star born of black
Be brighter than many stars born of white?

So what then?
You
Experts of color
Who define all
Even those who don't want to be defined
Redefine your colors
Also your stars
For this one over here
A chocolate star
That in your world is non-existent
Exists even against your will

Even if you remain quiet
You have heard my message

So,
I go
Smiling

Poet the Painter

If painting is all about mixing colors
Different colors of paints
And poetry is about mixing words
Different words to make meaning
Then a poet is a painter
And a painter is a poet

If painting is about making wonderful designs
Designs that can steal away the minds of passers-by
And poetry is about making meaningful phrases out of
wonderfully joined words
Phrases that can steal away the minds of the readers
Then painting is writing poetry
And writing poetry is painting

If painting is about making something more visible
Visible to the eyes of those who didn't care much to see what
is there
And poetry is about making something clearer and more
visible
Clearer and more visible to those who didn't think seriously
about the subject of poetry
Then painting is poetry
And poetry is painting
If a painter paints a house for the people to see
Painting reveals
And a poet writes poetry for the people to read other
people's minds
Poetry reveals
Then a painter is a poet

And a poet is a painter

If a painter is a creator of images
Painting creates images with a bite
It exhales things into being
And if a poet is a creator of images
Poetry creates images with a bite
It exhales things into being

Then who am I?
A poet or a painter?
But they say I am poet the painter

Reality of Things

Rain can beat a leopard's skin
But does it have the power enough to wash her spots?

Children can play with lion's young at home
But does they the power to tame its lioness?

A buffalo is a great animal in a jungle where there are no elephants
But is it a great animal in a jungle where there are elephants?

A king has the power to command his servants to obey him
But does he have the power to command hunger not to gnaw him?

A strong and hearty soldier fights fiercely in a battle
But can he fight fiercely to live forever?

Deep waters can be calm and silent
But do they spare a mischievous child who tests their depths with both feet?

The sword of a warrior is designed to fight an enemy
But does it spare the owner when it is directed towards his mouth?

A frog likes water
But does it like the water even when it is boiling?

Wealth is a good thing to have
But isn't it that virtue is much better?

Flowers of a tree produce fruits
But do all the flowers in a tree produce fruits?

Duck seeks water
But isn't it that some birds avoid water?

A one-eyed man may thank God
But isn't it that he will thank God even more when he sees a
man who is totally blind?

A storyteller tell stories
But isn't it that he cannot tell everything he knows?

It is good to travel with a companion
But isn't it much better to travel alone than to travel with a
bad companion?

A man can manage to burn his own house
But isn't it that he cannot manage to conceal the smoke that
comes thereupon?

A many can say something over a dead lion's body
But isn't it that he cannot afford to say something over a
lively lion's body?

Wood can stay a decade long in water
But isn't it that it cannot change into a crocodile?

Forehead and backside exist on the same head
But isn't it that they can never meet?

Cactus is bitter
But isn't it that it's not bitter even to him who doesn't taste
it?

A woman can kindle fire
But isn't it that if she licks or sets her foot on it she will burn
herself?

A blade is sharp
But isn't it that it cannot cut another blade?

A priest can sing "Halleluia" everywhere
But isn't it that this does not prove his piety?

Hard questions that crack the teeth
Digest

Runaway Voyages

When shall you settle your mind?
When shall you return from your runaway voyages?
When shall you re-enter your motherland?
When shall you re-unite with your fatherland?

Like the adventurous men's futile journey of escape into the
space
Like the adventurous men's futile dreams to find an empty
planet
Like the adventurous men's futile attempt to escape from
mother and humanity
Your journeys are uncertain wonderings

How long the journeys will take, you know not
How long the journeys will cost, you know not
Whether the journeys will be a real success, you know not
A life of uncertainties

When shall you seek re-entry?
When shall you seek re-union?
When shall you settle your mind?

Your voyages are all runaway ancestors
They are like the adventurers of Odysseus
They are like the explorations of Cecil John Rhodes
They are like the voyages of Vasco da Gama
They are like the war adventures of Alexander the Greek
They are like adventures of spacecrafts running away earth

Listen now, listen
Your voyages are nothing more than runaway ancestors
Your explorations are nothing more than rebellions of a child
to its mother
Your adventures are nothing more than a running away horse
 Come home, therefore, come home
And re-negotiate your re-entry
And re-negotiate your re-union
And rethink your present-future
And even your past-present
Come home, therefore, come home

The Beggar's Confessions

If they are real Christians
They know
That hatred is sinful
That hard heartedness is sinful
That love is Godly

For a decade now
I stand here
By the gate of the synagogue
My poor wooden plate by my side
My only friend

I see them
When they pass
Tying hard their pockets
Lest
What they spared for the church offering might fall
And poor Beggar might feast on it

With the corner of an eye
Some look
Scornfully
That for good I desert the gate
My home
To where?
Only them know better

Now after this decade long
My ten years of befriending the gate
My home

I know who Christian is
What it means to be a Christian

Christians are not those who preach Christ on top of their voices
Christians are not those who frequent the synagogue every Sunday
Christians are not those who wear church uniforms in the streets
Christians are not those who hold and read the Bible on the road

For what they really believe in
If a vagrant in the shaky behind the rich Christians' house die from hunger in their presence
If a beggar at the gate of the feasting synagogue lives there with dry lips
If brethren spare for a church uniform when the beggar by their gate lives in tattered rugs
If what the church can only afford to offer is the Holy Communion?
Then our entire path is littered with thorns

Mine is a voice of reason
Confessions of a beggar
Food for thought for all Christian fellows
Though unsweetened sour words for those who hate the truth
Amen!

By the Namahacha Waters

Deep in the jungles of Namahacha
The land of the sacred
Seated
Only a few inches from the fountainhead of the sacred waters
Its reflections clear as moonlight
Its foams white as the snow of the Arctic

Down the stream
A majestic creature of mother water
Its head a beautiful angel
Its tail a big glaring fish
A human-fish!

At first
Fear grip

Then,
My spirit jostles before,
A chuckle in my face
As human-fish beckons
Inviting me for a votive feast
With a smile in her face

Off the wind
I went
To join a confederal communion
And the goddess of rendering
Only to come back
To tell this tale

Voice of Concern

How painful it is to a hen to have its eggs of hope plundered by the leg of an elephant?

How painful it is to an eagle to have its one and only egg rotten by rain water?

How painful it is to a casualty to see his fellow friend putting salt on his wounds?

How painful it is to the owner of property to be defeated by a thief?

How painful it is to the faithful to contract HIV/Aids when the infidels walk away freely?

How painful it is to the innocent when they are convicted and the guilty are freed?

How painful it is to the industrious to get poorer when the indolent counterpart gets even richer?

How painful it is to the just to witness injustice prevails over justice even in the courts of law?

How painful it is to the lovers of peace to see war being waged against them and their will?

How painful it is to the deserving winners to see their losers win merit awards?

Mine is a voice of concern

A voice of reason

That haunts him who has thoughts in fetid syntax

Consider it!

Cosmetic Education

Everywhere education is ideally a liberator
Everywhere education is ideally an emancipator
Everywhere education is ideally a civilizing agent
Everywhere education is ideally a source of happiness
Everywhere education is ideally a cultivator of human culture

But what is the value of education
That is foreign to its people
That embraces only foreign culture
That decimates mother values
That emphasizes mimicry and castigates creativity
That devalues value systems of its people
That shatters the liberation of those it attracts
That enslaves those it purports to represent
That instead of teaching mocks the other
That privileges unequal encounters
That silence critiques through imposition
That is rigidly one-dimensional
That cherishes prescriptiveness and discredits flexibility
That discredits and pays no attention to alternative voices?

Confused World

Ours is a confused world
A world where daylight nudity is now celebrated
A world where elders are now disrespected
A world where God is now replaced by human intelligence
A world where everything good is now attributed to fortune
A world where human ability is now accredited for every achievement
A world where success is now attributed to human wisdom

Ours is a confused world
A world where children crying for water are now given beer
A world where those who are ill are now wished to die
A world where hospitals now prescribe drugs that are found nowhere in the market
A world where many have now become poor impoverished by the few filthy rich
A world where the few rich refuse to share with beggars
A world where collectivism have now been substituted by individualism
A world where everything West is now considered the best even if it is the worst
Ours is a confused world!

Do you Really Love Me?

If you really love me
Why did you enslave my people?
Why did you colonize my people?
Why did you sell my people firearms?
Why did you categorically terrorize my people?
Why are you against my rebellious people?

If you really love me
Why do you continue plundering my cultures in the false name of civilization?
Why do you continue dominating my systems in the false name of globalization?
Why do you continue imposing your nefarious theories that perpetuate inequality?
Why do you continue imposing your economic systems that devour my economies?

If you really love me
Why do you continue stealing away my talented sons and daughters?
Why do you continue sponsoring wars in exchange of my mineral resources?

If you really love me
Why derogatory statements made against my people are still printed on the walls of your palaces?
Why derogatory false statements claimed by your sons and daughters are still printed in the pages of your books?
Why the names of your false heroes are still printed on road signposts of my land?

If you really love me
Why do you still play hide and seek with my people?
Why do you still preach hypocrisy to my people?
Why do you still preach peace with a dirty tongue?
Why do you still sign peace accords with guns and not pens?
When you know that oil cannot extinguish fire
And that war cannot stop another war
And that you cannot dig a pit to fill another pit
And that you cannot correct one wrong by another wrong?

Capitalism

Capitalism
The worst enemy of the poor
The worst enemy of lovers of equality and equity
An imperial baby
Cunning and treacherous

With capitalism slavery was born
With capitalism colonialism was born
With capitalism world wars were born
The worst enemy of lovers of peace

Capitalism
With capitalism social inequality was born
With capitalism domineering was born
With capitalism expansionist policies were born
With capitalism racial exploitation was born
With capitalism, money- the source of all evil- was born

Capitalism
With capitalism the ideology of racism was born
With capitalism the ideology of apartheid was born
With capitalism the ideology of money economy was born

Capitalism
With capitalism resources were siphoned off
From the colonized to the colonizer
From black to white
From Africa to Europe
From the worker to capitalist
From India to Europe

Capitalism
What good then has you brought us the majority?
Mechanization?
Money economy?
What?

Thigh Vendors

Through what they manufacture not nor purchase they
survive
Through dirty works of their hands they feed

Thigh vendors!
They know neither morality nor fidelity
They know no boundary so long money

Thigh vendors!
Their love places long streets of Main Avenue
Their area of specialization
Self-taught horizontal gymnastics they never studied at school
For their classroom is bedroom

Thigh vendors!
They listen to no teaching
They heed to no advice
They consider no preaching
Their gospel only preached in the bar

Thigh vendors!
Their morals defy the logic of reason
Their ideas defy the highest level of imagination
For their behavior is all contrary to the logic of culture

Thigh vendors!
They fear neither pandemic nor accident
Neither men nor God
For their god is money
And disease Vaseline to smear
Only to die a miserable death

The Day Coming

I see the walls of the world shivering like reeds in winter
The flour of the earth shaking and quacking as the day approaches

I see the world staggering like a drunkard in the moonless night
Missing the width size of the path house as the day approaches
I see big mountains racing from west to east and from north to south
Seeking deliverance of Him and only Him as the day approaches

I see deep waters of the sea wondering in confusion
All in fear of judgment against the lives they swallowed and devoured as the day approaches

I see the pillars of the kings' palaces shaking in reverberation
Crumbling upon each other as deafening sound of the thunderous trumpet blows as the day approaches

I see the mouth of the hungry lions opening wider than the mouth of a pair of scissors
Only to devour those that resisted His will as the day approaches

I see the skeletal pieces of long dead bones reassembling in the precision of a maker
Joining to form yet another being that disappeared on the face of the earth as the day approaches

PhD

Some say: 'It's permanent head damage'
Others say: 'It's press her down'
More others say: 'It's pull him down'
For the harder you try to climb up
The more others try hard to pull you down
Such that it becomes a journey up and up
A tree one cannot afford to climb with hands in the pocket

PhD
A long journey it is
Winding as it spirals up
Staggering upwards slowly like smoke in a still day
That is never certain if it will ever get to the ozone
But they keep on saying:
'Go! Go! Go on….'
They say to the ceiling
Of what?
I know not what

PhD
It takes not only courage
To climb up such a tree smeared with okra
A tree thorny all its trunk up
But real commitment bartered with hard work
And hard work nurtured with intelligence and wits

PhD
A test of time and not only for the psyche
That like death is feared by many
That like a vicious lion leaves many with bruises

That like a fierce battle leaves many with injuries
Physical, psychological or spiritual
I know not what

Big Brother

Playhouses were everything
Then you taught me how set trapping stones for mice
And you set a stone for me across the mice path
To expect a catch on the morrow

You were short and I was tall and thin
And your boyish, smart tricks was the prize I had to win
If I were to be wiser than you or at least speak the same
language as you did

Way, way beyond my bedding time
Flat stones balanced on my head
Heading towards our rich planting field

Now, I search for mice path myself
With expertise of a medical doctor in diagnosing a disease
Remembering all the tips and words you taught
Making sure your voice is never lost or dies
For it filled my ears
The knowledge all my head
And the tactics all my body

Childhood in Village

The sweetness of youth is sweeter than honey
Twice as good as adult life:
The unconditional laughters, the happiness
All plays, simple
All faces the epicenters of joy
The passion – mimicry and creativity

All contributing to positive growth;
Of the soul, of the mind and of body
As a backed cake, roasted in oven
With all ingredients for it to taste

We all long to recline
To the hey days of youths
To the train of adventures
That like a chameleon moves slowly but sure of the steps
To nourish the psyche and the spirit
And to manure and water the body

Playhouse

Mother is my name
Theirs are father, grandma, grandpa, grandson,
granddaughter, and children
A complete family bound by the forces of communalism and
collectivism

We cook together
We share all our food
We work together
We share the fruit of our sweat
All in the name of collectivism

I watch as the sunrise
With a broom in my hand
My waist wrapped in *kapulana*
My head in the head gear, *dhuku*
I work, I work,
As I watch my children playing

At midmorning I am there playing with my cooking sticks
Gourd is my washing dish
Strychnos cocculoides gourds my plates
All my children round in circle
For a communion meal

False Dawn

When they went out of scene all of us were happy
But that was our folly for little did we know:
That a young one of a snake is also a snake
That everywhere baboons are the same

We were all thirsty for justice
But where is justice our dear friend
When courts of law set the most wanted suspects on bail?
When police dine with the most notorious criminals on the land?
When kings of corruption move freely in the streets?
When 'fraudsters' pocket millions of dollars of desperate home seekers yet still held unaccountable for their crimes?
When arrogance and cruelty of those at the helm increases day by day?
When the feelings of those in struggle for good life are thwarted without excuse?
Trodden under feet,
Like a hand thwarting a mosquito against the wall
False dawn!

Africa the Betrayed Continent

Like sheep in wolves' skins they came
Like a python luring its prey they behaved

Disturbing peace of peace loving Africa
Setting her at the edge of a cultural precipice
Translating their opportunities into difficulties for the sons
and daughters of the soil
Endangering the continent willy-nilly
Threatening all its humanity into nonentity
Silencing the voiceless
Only to shatter their hopes

Though welcomed with both hands
And the people poised for a faithful kiss
Theirs was a deceitful kiss
Forged in broad daylight

Moonlight Shadow

Heated argument it was
So heated it left bruises in both our hearts
And footprints of pain in our consciousness

The argument started from the moonlight shadow
I was saying it was a human being approaching us
He was saying it's a donkey, big
She was saying it's a night ghost

For an hour we argued
The shadow stuck and unmoved
In that forest path to Wenela

A bad omen
We all thought
But Alas!
What to do?

Mob Violence, the Maputo Way

They say it's mob violence
The mob says it's mob justice

Hear the complaints of the mob:
'We have listened more than enough to these 'Order Order
men'
The ones who say don't take the law in your hands
The ones who say all crimes should be reported to police
Thieves
Rapists
Murderers
They take long to execute justice
Backlogs in the courts'

Now hear the mob, their justice:
'Our justice never delays
It descends faster than summer lighting
Determined
You steal a goat we cut your arms
You rape a child we send your mischievous whip to the dogs
You murder a fellow being we bath you in petrol
Or smolder you in car tyres
You drive recklessly and run over somebody we beat you and
burn your car
You shoot somebody the next second you are in hell
You plunder state coffers, hey beware!
You will journey alone beyond the cosmos
Our justice is vicious but fast and efficient
No backlog'

Wishes of a Good Child

Riches are good but not the best of all that men can live by
Cash
Houses
Cars
Cell phones
All are signs of a good living
But not the best of all that men can live by

Rather,
I wish to grow up a happy persona
I wish to grow up a wise persona
I wish to grow up a loving persona
I wish to grow up a God fearing persona
For these are the best that men can live by

Long Gone Ever Present

The dead have gone
Long gone
But ever present

When I am seated
Alone in the forest
I hear their voices
Sweet

My eyes too blind to see
I just hear the echoes
Scratching myself to make sure I am awake
Not foraging in the dreamland far away

When I sleep
My mind prowling all over
I see them by the key hole
Peeping
Sometimes by the window
Listening to my night breathe

When a war break in their house
Even a match of some sort
They ask me and everyone else to participate
The old
The young
The sick
The strong
Women
Men

All sent to war for the cause they know not what .
For they are the only ones privileged to live in two worlds

Their requests
Like those of a comeback child
A sign that they were robbed of their love of mother earth
A sign that they can still rise above their agony
A sign that their attachment to the lovely little ones exist ever
Long gone ever present

Who doesn't wish?

Day come night go
Light come darkness go
Life come death go
Peace come war go
Love come hatred go
Happiness come sorrow go
Goodness come bad go
Friend come enemy go
Hope come hopelessness go
Health come disease go
Richness come poverty go
Who doesn't wish?

The Price of Ignorance

Too exorbitant a price!
For going out with him before knowing his status
I almost paid with a box with no space
For playing with fire before asking mom whether it burns
I paid with a cry - a deadly wound
For sitting in the exam before consulting my teachers and the
library
I paid with a failure, dismal
A heavy fine
The penalty that pained me all life

Now I stare as I see him
Descending
Pick pocketing
On the morrow
Before the magistrate
Five years behind bars
He cried:
'I didn't know this would send me here
Pardon me!'

From the other side of the road
I look
Him coming in his Blue Bird
Criss-crossing
Eh, he is drunk
That old woman in three legs
Struggling to cross over on her legs
He runs over
On the morrow

Before the magistrate
Twenty-five years of hard labor
He cried:
'I didn't know it's a crime to drink and drive
Pardon me!'

Just across the road
I see
Two students in uniforms
Brown bottles in their hands
Staggering
By the school gate they vomit
Only foam
Before the school Head
Expulsion
They cried:
'We didn't know we shouldn't drink and come to school
Pardon us!'

On my left side – barely ten meters away
Melodrama!
A young man in his teen is quarreling with what appears to be
a friend
From his waist
A pistol!
He points to the friend
On the morrow
Before the magistrate
Seven years behind bars
He cried:
'I didn't know it's a crime to point a gun to a friend and in
the public

We were only playing and it had no bullets
Pardon me!'
All because of ignorance

16 Years of Horror

(For the 16 years civil war in Mozambique, 1975-1992)

I can't believe what I saw
Though my eyes were wide open
And in the daylight

My mind keeps on insisting
That I believe what I saw
Even my heart
For it overwhelms my heart and soul
Even that time
It was only body who endured to bear the truth

Surviving in horror is tough
For the memories of the long gone
Keep coming
Like the comeback kid
They keep on reminding
That I think of them
And feel for them
Against those odds and evils that doomed their bodies

I am forced to remember that fateful day
In my grandmother's village
Her real home
Yes
A toddler I still was
With milk on my nose
But the horror doesn't want to be forgotten

From the window of our tiny hut
I saw them coming
All with what appeared to be AKs
Knives and canisters all over their bodies

Knowing the reality of danger
Grandma fitted in our poor wooden cage
Tattered rugs all over the cage
I heard her uttering what seemed a silent prayer to the whale
of the sea
To come and do what it did to Jonah

How they discovered her
I don't know
All what I know
They never dared asking anything
But of their own volition
Separated her goodness from me
Her soul they took away
And off they went

Death of the Village Preacher

The village is quiet
Only funeral dirges
Gourds of tears
All broken
The village preacher is dead!

The village preacher is dead!
The village preacher who warned of the impending drought
The village preacher who rebuked the elephant when it
plundered the poor man's hut
The village preacher who criticized the elephant for frittering
away the village coffers
The village preacher who revealed the elephant's lie
The village preacher who preached peace that year war broke
out
The village preacher is dead

The village preacher is dead!
Why did he die?
Did he deserve this untimely death?
Can't you death restore the life you have stolen away?
Don't you know the village preacher deserves no death?

The village preacher is dead!
Now the elephant will plunder the poor men's huts without
shame
Now the elephant will lie without shame
Now the village planners will squander the village coffers
without recourse

Now the warlords will wedge war against the innocent
without shame

The village preacher is dead!
Who will rebuke the elephant?
Who will shame the elephant?
Who will catch up with the elephant?

The village preacher is dead!
Because the village preacher was a man of truth
Now the village is gone
Only its gourds of tears will remain
Flowing like the waters of the Nile
Marking the good works of the village preacher

Before Winter Swallows Summer

Before winter swallows summer
Gather everything protective
Ahead of harsh weathers to come
For there shall be no time
To go out in bad weather

Before night swallows day
Gather many sticks for a bonfire
For the night shall be longer than usual
And there shall be no time
To go out at night
To gather more sticks

But a question for you:
Would you be happy if winter is dead
That summer comes
And comes to stay?
Or
Would you celebrate if night is kidnapped
That day comes
And comes to stay?
Or
Would you weep like a child whose sweet is taken away from
his mouth
That summer and winter, night and day
Should alternate?

I once asked the youth these questions
They only looked at me
Dumbfounded

I then asked the elders
They all said: 'Madness- These are the rantings of a madman
You better go where you were bewitched
To hell with your stupid questions'

I then went to the wise
They all said: 'Man!
Come, sit here!
And let's discuss this matter
But meanwhile you better write a poem
Then
We discuss the matter'

And even today
We are still discussing

Child Love

Voice: When I was a child
Chorus: Yes
I loved everyone
Yes

When I was a child
Yes
Even to my enemies
Yes
I smiled
Yes
Not a treacherous smile
Yes
But a faithful smile
Yes

When I was a child
Yes
Even to those witches
Yes
Who planned to feast on me
Yes
I waved in love
Yes

When I was a child
Yes
I didn't know
Yes
That

Growing up
Yes
Deprives
Yes
Me
Yes
Of my faithful love
Yes
That ever since
Yes
Was unconditional
Yes

Now
Yes
That I realize
Yes
The folly of growth
Yes
I long
Yes
To go back
Yes
To my mother's womb
Yes

But
Yes
When I come back
Yes
I tell you
Yes

I would not want
Yes
To grow
Aaaaaaaaaaaaaaa!

Beware!

Beware of what might befall you
Judgment
But perhaps misjudgment

Serial killers
Murderers
Exterminators of life
Young and old

Even those of you
Who kill with guns and injections
You can't get away with it that easy
As you foolish yourselves through stupid imagination
For killing is killing

And worse still the insane murderers
Killers of the innocent – they say unwanted children
Unwanted by whom?
And who are you to decide for the unwanted?
Beware!

Even you
Wizards and witches – cannibals
Who feast on human flesh
You will not be spared
Perhaps if you repent
And leave your old ways

And you
Dictators

Who rule with a sword
Where is your peace,
The peace you promised your people?
Beware!

Lucifer is there
Like a thief in the dark
Waiting
His kiln is ready hot
His fork ready sharp
His energy ready invigorated
Also enraged by your numbers
You are too many a people!

Singing Rage of the Indian Ocean

It is not the advancing tide of the Indian Ocean
That compels me to sing this song
Nor the radiance of the waves of the ocean in summer
That compels me to open my mouth
Not even the waves of the ocean crashing to the shore
That compels me to speak

It is not the echoes of the tides of the Indian Ocean
That makes me cry
Nor the triumphal arterial of the ocean in summer
That makes me drop my tears

The spirit of love deep down the labyrinth of my heart
Compels
The spirit that longs ocean and land to marry
To procreate together
Not to enter into a contract of war
Compels

I have observed it many times
That
When ocean sings his rage
The fertile carrier of land shrivel of her parallax power
Trembling
Like a fearful dog
Its tail directs down – beneath
But ocean appears to be merciless even to those who have
surrendered
He plunders without concern
He obliterates without compassion

'Who shall go out there
To plead with the raging sea?'
Asked land one of those days
But all her councilors were cowards
No one volunteered
So,
The rage of ocean continues

John
(For my cousin brother, John)

Though it is good to be written and read
When you join the line to ancestors
It is even better to be written and read
When your body and spirit still hold on to each other
For the good
It encourages
For the bad
It teaches

Over to you
John
For the works of your own hands
And the revealed thoughts of your own spirit

Far be that you
Strangled with distance
My mind searches unceasingly
Soul searching
For the spring of your works
Good works

With your works
I am convinced when the adage goes:
'Teachers are born not bred'
To us all
You are a teacher who was born not bred

For those of us who follow you
Your works never tire

To yield
Hope
Success
And happiness

When I learnt of the news
Breaking news!
That they have stolen away your partner
Your eye at work – Nyemu
All our gourds were torn
Asunder
To émigré the hidden waters – tears
Until when
We cannot tell
For the gourds are perennial

But cry not brother
Cry not without hope
For every event has a reason for its cause
Your good works
Her good works
Your everlasting wonderful lessons
Her everlasting wonderful lessons
They were all seeds sown on the fertile land
One day is one day
They will sprout – emerge
And grow
To replace the cemetery of hopelessness that the devil has
sown
Deep in the labyrinth of your heart

My message
Small but great
Let hope flourishes forever in you
For what was stolen from you shall be replaced
When the time comes

When People Want to Speak

When people want to speak
The will of their hearts
It is like smoke of a burning house
It cannot be concealed

When people want to speak
The will of their hearts
It is like a full tight balloon
It cannot be pressed under water

I have seen it in Rome
I have seen it in China

I have seen it in the Americas
I have seen it in Egypt

I have seen it in Philippines
I have seen it in Malawi

I have seen it in Togo
I have seen it elsewhere

Where bad governance prevails
Also lies, deception and propaganda exist
I can't leave out larceny and kleptocracy
For together they are the spices
That set democracy under fire
And destroy the will of the people

While the despot do everything possible

To consolidate his power
To repress criticism
To chase forbidden longings in hot pursuit of undue fame
To give himself a leg up on competition
Even where the stone hungers for a change
The will of the people will not weary

No matter how long it may take
For the will of the people to be printed on the walls of the
white house
No amount of force
Nor strength of a dictator
Even political moth, rust, and temerity
Will ever be able to rule without the people's consent forever

Where poor governance yields
The rulers shall expect to reap in obscurity
Bedlam
Tribulation
And even orgies and parties when ousted
But where good governance prevails
Excellence
And prominence

The Power of Poetry

They think nothing but violence
When they eat - even feasting
They do so to nourish their energies
To execute violence par – excellence

Now let the poet speak
Though they say words do not kill
Now let the poet cry
Though they say the poet's cry do not bring back the dead
Now let the poet sing
Though they say the song of a poet is like an ant on the back
of an elephant
Now let the poet breathe
Though they say the breathe of a poet is like still wind in the
desert
Now let the poet spit on their works
Though they say the saliva of a poet is like a drop of oil in the
ocean

One day is one day
The words of a poet
Shall kill he who do not believe
The cry of a poet
Shall bring back the long departed
The song of a poet
Shall overwhelm the elephant of the land
The breathe of a poet
Shall blow away the elephant like a mosquito in the whirlwind
The saliva of a poet

Shall diffuse all the waters of the ocean like a drop of
raspberry in a glass of water

Because flesh no matter of which animal
Will bleed when cut
Because elephant no matter how big it is
Will suffer pain and loss
Because elephant no matter how heavy it is
Will feel the effect of the wind
Because water no matter how much it is
Will feel the presence of oil
Such is the power of poetry

Distance

Yesterday I didn't know
That distance hurts even those who love her
That distance kills even those who smile at her

I have been watching for some time now
The cunning steps of distance
That it behave like wind who asks mosquito to accompany her to some place
Mosquito thinking wind will accompany him back to where he took him

I have been watching for some time now
The treacherous tricks of distance
That like a hungry python plays glitters to prey
The prey thinking it has met a best friend ever since

Her works?
Dirty!

Five years down the line she sent Peter the father of four to the Americas
Back home his family she torn apart

Four years down the line she sent Joseph the betrothed to England
Back home her betrothed girlfriend she betrothed yet to another man

Three years down the line she sent the best friends of the land - Manuel and Daniel

One to Canada and the other to Japan
In a month's time she had destroyed their friendship

Two years down the line she sent Tapita to Australia
Back home his relationship with his parents she killed

Now, I hear the news in the city
Rumours
That she has recently sent Tamanda to Holland
Leaving behind his wife
I fear for them
I fear!

In Gorongoza Forest

It was my two dogs and I
Together in the forest
Myself whistling the totemic praises of my long gone fathers
Atop the morning dew of June
Searching for the red boy of the left hand

A few meters into the heart of the forest
Alas!
My God!
The king of the jungle
Hidden under the gazing African morning sun

The silence that followed answered with a whisper
Fine but strong
Collected memories of my departed grandfather trickling in
'Don't run
Look him right in the eyes if you meet him'
I remembered
My heart playing *mbakumba*
A dance that leaves one tired and sweating

My dogs – my companion boys!
A sigh of relief
Machena and Chikara wagging their virile tails
Emerging from the back of the king of the jungle

Stealing away the attention of the king
He faced my boys –Machena and Chikara
For a moment
Playing a matador's fearful dance with the bull

His finger nails playing an untold story on my boys

I only remember holding tight – clinging
To a branch at the zenith of a *Diospyros mespiliformis*
How I got there
Only fortune
To tell this incredible tale
But my boys now history

Troubled Mother Earth

My heart
All wounds
Bleeding
Weeping
For ozone my friend
Crying
For mother earth my sister
And her loving daughters
River
Forest
And atmosphere

I plead
Day and night
To ears that never hear
To eyes that never see
To hearts that never feel

They listen not when I tell them the news
That ozone layer is now all holes
Broken
That thick rain forest over there is now history
That the water in that river is now tea with milk
That the grounds by the city are now pain in the neck
Havens of rats where all, big and small, hold their meetings
even during the day
Hives of flies where all, small and the green bombers, hold
their rallies all day

Only yesterday
I told them breaking news
That the other forest by the river is only smoke that staggers
skywards
Threatening mother earth a lifeless burnt cinder
Poisoning the very air they share with all others
But their ears
All concrete

They seem not to care
As the mindless zombies of the desert

They exploit as if they will all die today
They burn as if they breathe only smoke
They pollute water as if they bathe not
They harvest as if they want to migrate to another planet
today
Troubling our mother earth

Is this not our common heritage
Mother earth
That with glean hope
God endowed with all treasure?

The Hard Hit Drought

(In memory of the 1992 drought in Southern Africa)

Days of hot dry air accumulated into weeks
Into fortnights and into months
All:
People,
Plants,
Animals,
And even the mother earth
Waiting for the rain

In what used to be a thick forest
I watched
Trees bowing down their heads in grief as they pray for
deliverance
Their roots, trunks, branches and leaves
All dressed in sorrow as they thirsty and hunger for life

In the fields
I watched helplessly
As I saw Master Farmers' scores of months of hard labour
wasted
Reduced to spittle dust
Their monies buried to rot as if was a sacrifice to mother
earth
Leaving them with gloom hope and heads bowed in sorrow
All in one prayer
'God, why have you forsaken us?'

In the sky
The sun had fought its fierce wicked battle against cloud

It was all blue from east to west, north to south
Even the Zaire-Congo winds could not garner the courage to
enter the ring
To fight sun the ruthless warrior
For trees and birds had refused to form allies with them to
fight sun

With a hopeless heart
I carried my mosquito body down to the weeping forest
Not to console her but to add salt to her bleeding wounds
Digging fiercely her desperate roots
Wicked sun watching
With a smile in his face

God forbid
Even sun must have mercy on us
We couldn't resist
The thinking that Lucifer had grabbed the keys of heaven
from the angel of rain and ran mad
To starve the people and force them into his kingdom

Only after several months of desperate waiting
Perhaps when the angel of God got hold of him, he who had
stolen away the keys
That is when we saw wind now cooperating
Clouds in action – in real combat
Uniformed
Plants dancing unceasingly
Whistling and ululating to encourage wind and cloud not to
lose hope
At last sky was pregnant
Then it happened

Spoiled Child

A toddler
I was spoiled
Deceived from the start by she who gave me milk
Chewing for me
Treating me like a golden egg
Yet beckoning harbingers of lethargy and bad lucky

In me false hope was sown
Only castles in the air
Built
In me pseudo packages of success were tasselled
Only to reach stunted growth before noon

Forty years later
On this lonely road I wane
I remain a child amidst peers
With nothing to show except age
All my blessings ran away mad
Escorting indolence

As usual the morning sun rises
To bring me nothing but dazzling reality
Compelling me to accept all it brings without choice
Even the ugly images of poverty I receive
Even the incredible packages of smokescreen I receive
For I no longer know what is good for me

I,
Mr Lonely the deserted
All friends,

My wife,
My children,
Have left years, years ago
Leaving behind me, Mr Lonely
Suffering untold hardships that even his ancestors never
tasted

In me they saw nothing but a nebulous whirlwind
Lost in the outlandish cadence scuffle of evil land
And fallen prey to pleonastic confusion
I am spoiled a child

Tanuka was her name

In the interior village of Tamazu
Lived a beatific 'princess', the forest blooming rose
Her name beautiful and unique
Tanuka the blooming rose

Tall and slender
She was
Her exquisiteness
A talking magic
A gossip of the birds of the forest
A free tourist attraction for the countless
An emblem of decoration
Yet the only daughter of Takapiwa and Tendai, the pitiable
old villagers

So loved was she the blooming rose
And so loving was she the blooming rose
All she had to do was to ask her parents
She would become the spring of their happiness
Their only God given treasure

The days that followed
Her plans she hatched
And grew to lure the son of the richest but humblest man on
the land

Then came the day
Nokito the well-heeled man's son
A well built, gorgeous and morally upright young man
Ambitious but reticent

Slow in action but wit and intelligent

After many arrows from all over the village had missed the
blooming rose
He made his way to the rose
Slow but sure of his steps
Lest he fall and miss the rose

There she is
As he sings his melodic song
She only nods
Nodding in approval
Her little heart running amok in traces of joy
Her eyes jerking,
Lyrics of hope looming
For she knew
This day will come
No need to rush

Together
In unison
They went
Only to come back treasure and happiness
What Tanuka had pledged